PIANO *Adventures*®

SCALE AND CHORD BOOK 2
One-Octave Scales and Arpeggios
by Nancy and Randall Faber

T0057126

This book belongs to: _____

Online Support
Scan the QR codes throughout the book
or visit **pianoadventures.com/qr/FF3025**

Production Coordinator: Jon Ophoff
Editor: Isabel Otero Bowen
Engraving: Dovetree Productions, Inc.

FABER
PIANO ADVENTURES®

ISBN 978-1-61677-662-6

Table of Contents

This chart will help you and your teacher track and celebrate each step of your progress.
Check or shade a box each time you have completed that practice activity.

SECTION 1

SECTION 2

SECTION 3

FF302

1-Octave Minor Flat Scales	natural minor	harmonic minor	melodic minor	primary chords	mini etude	challenge	trans-positions
A Minor.............................24						19, 20	
D Minor............................26						21	
G Minor............................28						22	
C Minor............................30						23	
F Minor 32						24, 25	
B♭ Minor 34						26, 27	
E♭ Minor...........................36						28	

SECTION 4

1-Octave Minor Sharp Scales	natural minor	harmonic minor	melodic minor	primary chords	mini etude	challenge	trans-positions
E Minor 38						29	
B Minor............................40						30	
F♯ Minor...........................42						31	
C♯ Minor 44						32	
G♯ Minor 46						33	

SECTION 5

1-Octave Minor Arpeggios	chromatically ascending	chromatically descending
Minor Arpeggios for R.H. 48		34
Minor Arpeggios for L.H. 50		35

SECTION 6

Chord Progressions and Harmony	by memory	transpositions	challenge
Pop Chord Etude 52			36
"Power Chord" Etude........................53			
"Classic" Cadence...........................54			37, 38
Happy Birthday – Harmony 55			
Happy Birthday – Melody 55			

SECTION 7

Note to Teacher

The Piano Adventures® Scale and Chord Books provide much more than a simple reference to scale fingerings and key signatures. The series develops essential pattern recognition by requiring transposition of carefully crafted exercises.

As follow-up to the 5-finger scales of Book 1, this book presents one-octave scales and arpeggios along with fundamental chord patterns. The Scale Routines present hands-alone and hands-together playing for keen listening and coordination. The Challenges develop important pattern recognition by exploring tonic (scale step 1), dominant (scale step 5), and leading tone (scale step 7) relationships in many keys.

One-octave arpeggios provide a technical workout using wrist circles while preparing for chord inversion mastery at the next level. The final section gives a practical orientation to the common chord progressions used in pop, folk, and classical music. The student's crowning achievement for this level is to accompany Happy Birthday in any key.

Scale Routine
Students often play scales hands-together too soon, sacrificing evenness of tone and expressive shaping of the line. The Scale Routines carry the student through hands-alone practice, hands-together in parallel and contrary motion, and close with a chord cadence.

- When playing hands-alone, give careful attention to expressive dynamics and evenness of tone.

- Continuing with hands-together, focus on evenness of rhythm.

- For the primary chord cadences, listen for clean pedaling.

Challenges
Approach each Challenge by finding the tonic, dominant, and leading tone of the key. The Challenges will help the student hear and recognize these scale steps and related patterns in many keys.

Transposition
Transposing the Challenges builds musicianship. It is not always easy, but is most definitely rewarding. Look for scale steps 1, 5, and 7 (tonic, dominant, and leading tone) in the exercise, then identify the same scale steps in the new key.

One-Octave Arpeggios
These provide fruitful opportunity to practice graceful wrist circles as presented in the Piano Adventures® Technique & Artistry series. These circles distribute the arm weight by aligning the hand over each finger. Relax the thumb and let the hand close, even through the octave extension.

Chord Progressions and Harmony
The final section provides a practical harmony workout to be transposed to all keys. The I, IV, V, and vi chords are presented in four settings on page 52, to be played straight through in all keys:

- I–IV–V–I with roots in the bass

- I–IV–V–vi with roots below the tonic

- The I–vi–IV–V "Beach Party" progression

- The popular I–V–vi–IV "Pachelbel" progression

A setting for "Power Chords" in minor keys (i–VII–VI–V) on page 53 is followed by the I–IV–V7 "Classic" Cadence and a variation based on an ascending bass line. This leads to harmony workouts for Happy Birthday, which can be transposed to the student's favorite keys.

FF302

How to Use This Book

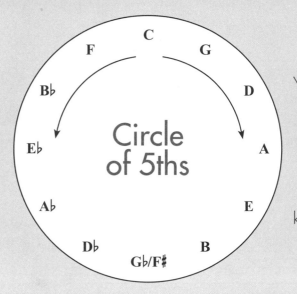

Circle of 5ths

You may progress through the book sequentially, from beginning to end, or you may work on several sections concurrently, with focus on only a few keys at a time. In other words, if you were exploring D and A major, you might study these scales in Section 1, these arpeggios in Section 3, and the chord progressions of Section 7 in these keys. Your teacher might also assign relative minor keys from Section 5.

All 12 major and 12 minor keys are presented in this book for full reference. Some students will appreciate studying all keys in depth; others may prefer to wait on the more difficult minor keys until Scale Book 3. All students should fully master the easier keys at this level, with transposition.

Transpose

Keep track of progress using the full chart on pages 2-3. To help track the many transpositions, a convenient chart is given for each Challenge.

C	G	D	A	E	B

1-Octave Major Sharp Scales

Memorize each Scale Routine and play without stopping.

Put a ✔ next to each tempo as you build speed.

_____ ♩= 96 _____ ♩= 144 _____ ♩= 192

C Major Scale Routine

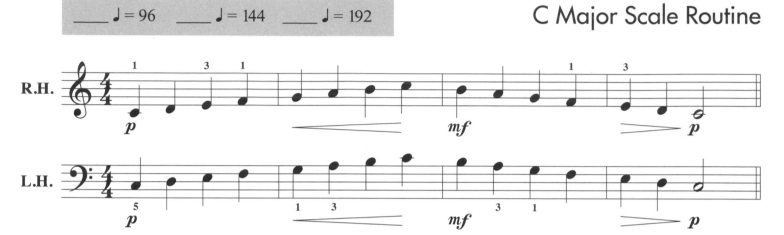

Parallel motion ... **Contrary motion**

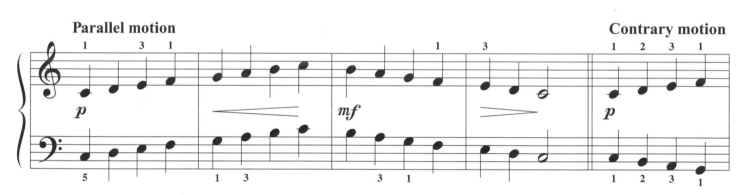

Primary chords

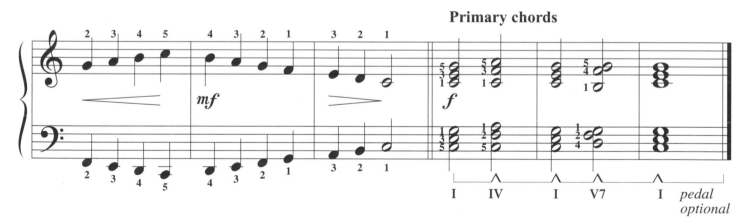

I   IV   I   V7   I   _pedal optional_

Challenge 1

f–p on repeat

Notice that the *last* sharp in a key signature is the **leading tone** (scale degree 7).
To name the key signature, go UP a *half step* from the leading tone (F♯ to G).

Challenge 2

Note the *leading tone* and the *dominant* (scale degree 5).

Transpose **Challenge 2** to C major and put a ✔ in the box when completed.

Remember that the *last* sharp in a key signature is the **leading tone** (scale degree 7).
To name the key signature, go UP a half step from the leading tone (C♯ to D).

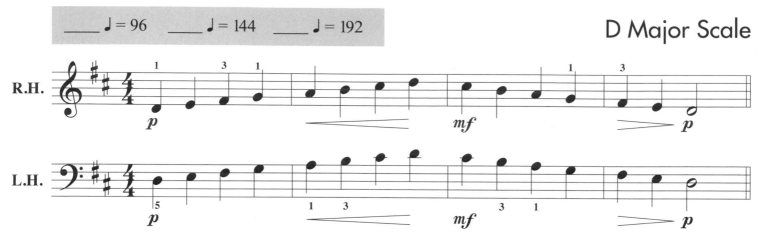

_____ ♩= 96   _____ ♩= 144   _____ ♩= 192

D Major Scale

Parallel motion   **Contrary motion**

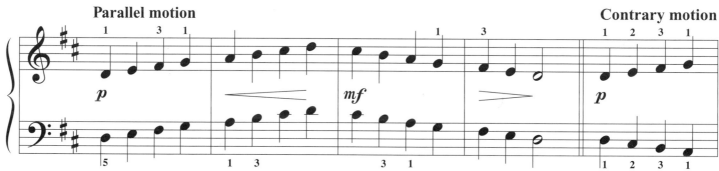

Primary chords

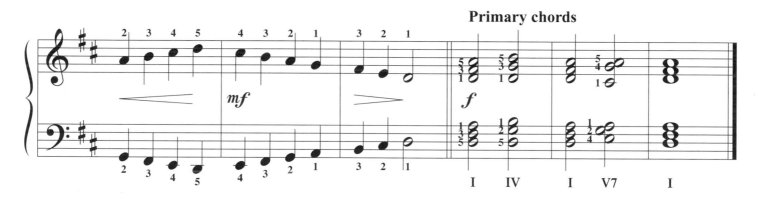

I   IV   I   V7   I

Challenge 3

dominant–tonic

f–p on repeat

dominant–dominant

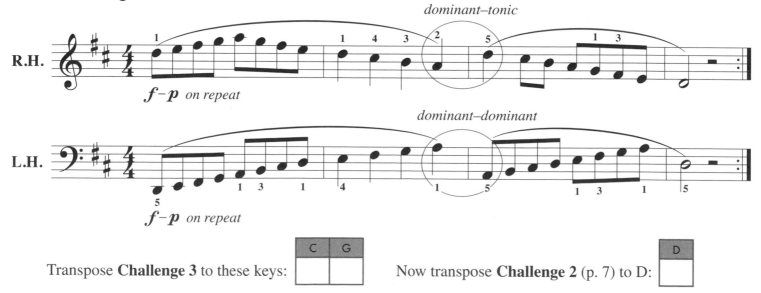

f–p on repeat

	C	G

D

Transpose **Challenge 3** to these keys: Now transpose **Challenge 2** (p. 7) to D:

FF302

Name the *last* sharp in the key signature: _____ #

Now go UP a half step. Did you land on A?

_____ ♩ = 96   _____ ♩ = 144   _____ ♩ = 192

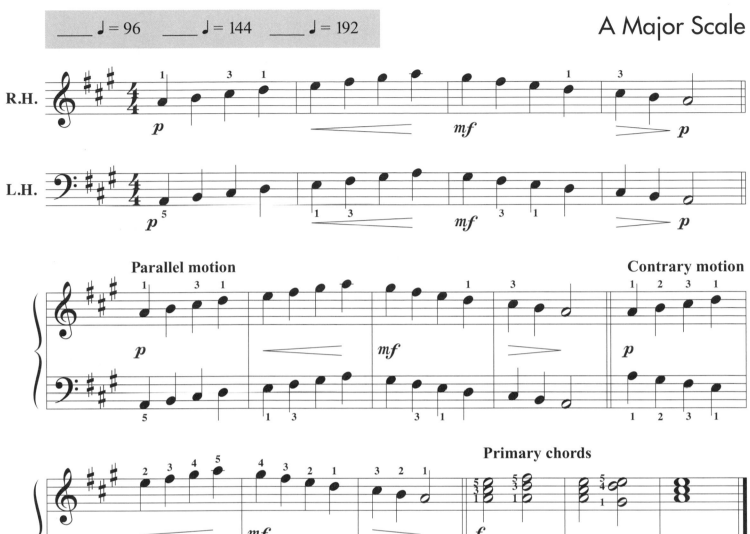

R.H.

L.H.

Parallel motion   **Contrary motion**

Primary chords

I   IV   I   V7   I

Challenge 4

The down-up arrows indicate circular wrist motions.

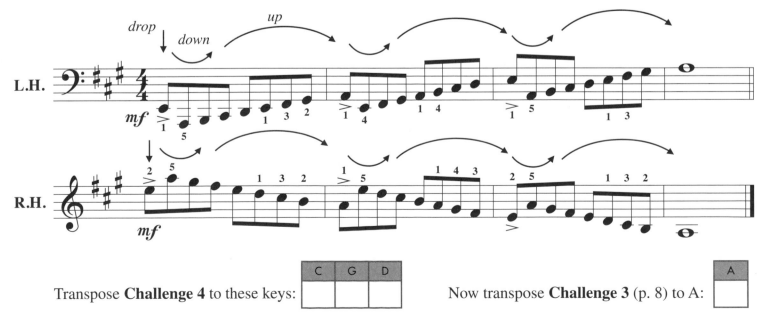

L.H.

R.H.

Transpose **Challenge 4** to these keys:

C	G	D

Now transpose **Challenge 3** (p. 8) to A:

A

Name the *last* sharp in the key signature: _____ #

Now go UP a half step. Did you land on E?

_____ ♩ = 96   _____ ♩ = 144   _____ ♩ = 192

E Major Scale

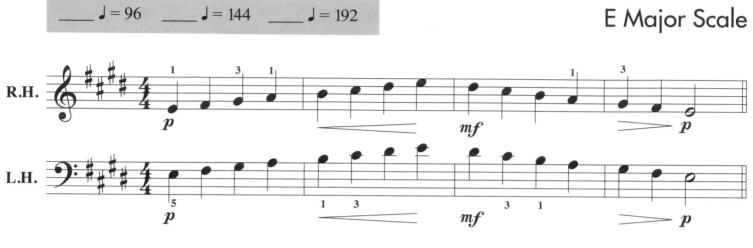

R.H.

L.H.

Parallel motion   **Contrary motion**

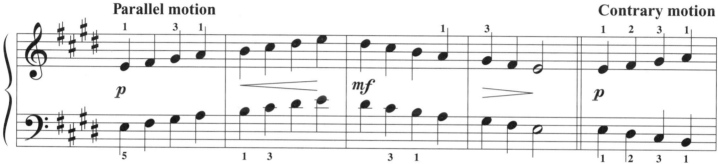

Primary chords

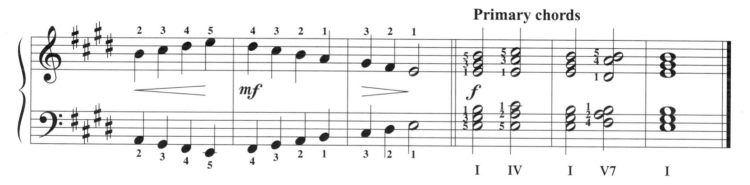

I   IV   I   V7   I

Challenge 5

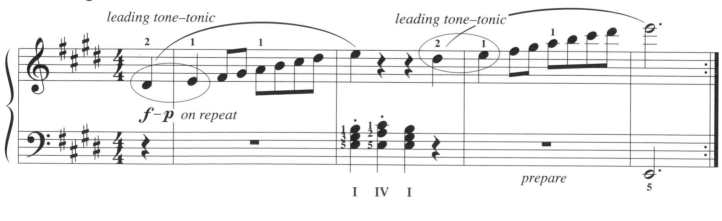

leading tone–tonic   *leading tone–tonic*

f–p on repeat

I   IV   I

prepare

C	G	D	A

Transpose **Challenge 5** to these keys:

Now transpose **Challenge 4** (p. 9) to E:

E

Name the *last* sharp in the key signature: ____ ♯
Now go UP a half step. Did you land on B?

____ ♩ = 96   ____ ♩ = 144   ____ ♩ = 192

B Major Scale

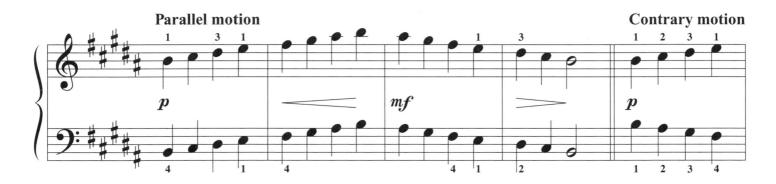

Parallel motion   **Contrary motion**

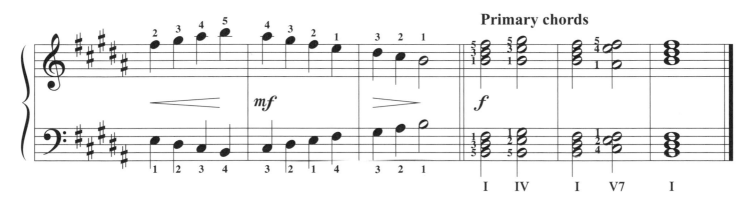

Primary chords

I   IV   I   V7   I

Challenge 6

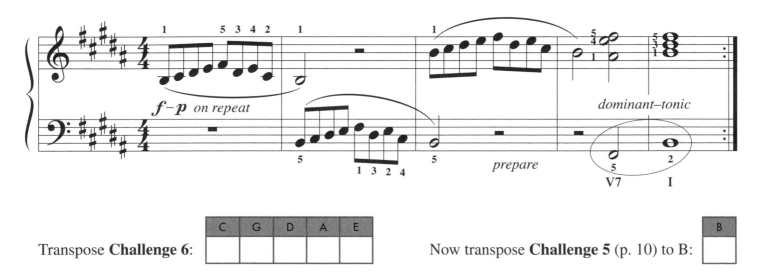

f–p on repeat

prepare

dominant–tonic

V7   I

	C	G	D	A	E			B

Transpose **Challenge 6**:   Now transpose **Challenge 5** (p. 10) to B:

Name the *last* sharp in the key signature: ____ #
Now go UP a half step. Did you land on F#?

____ ♩ = 96   ____ ♩ = 144   ____ ♩ = 192

F# Major Scale

Parallel motion

Contrary motion

Primary chords

I   IV   I   V7   I

Challenge 7

leading tone

Transpose **Challenge 7**.
How many keys can you do?

G	D	A	E	B

For the transpositions, begin with finger 1 and cross over with finger 2 for the *leading tone*.

As you play and transpose, watch for the *dominant, tonic,* and *leading tone*.

Challenge 8

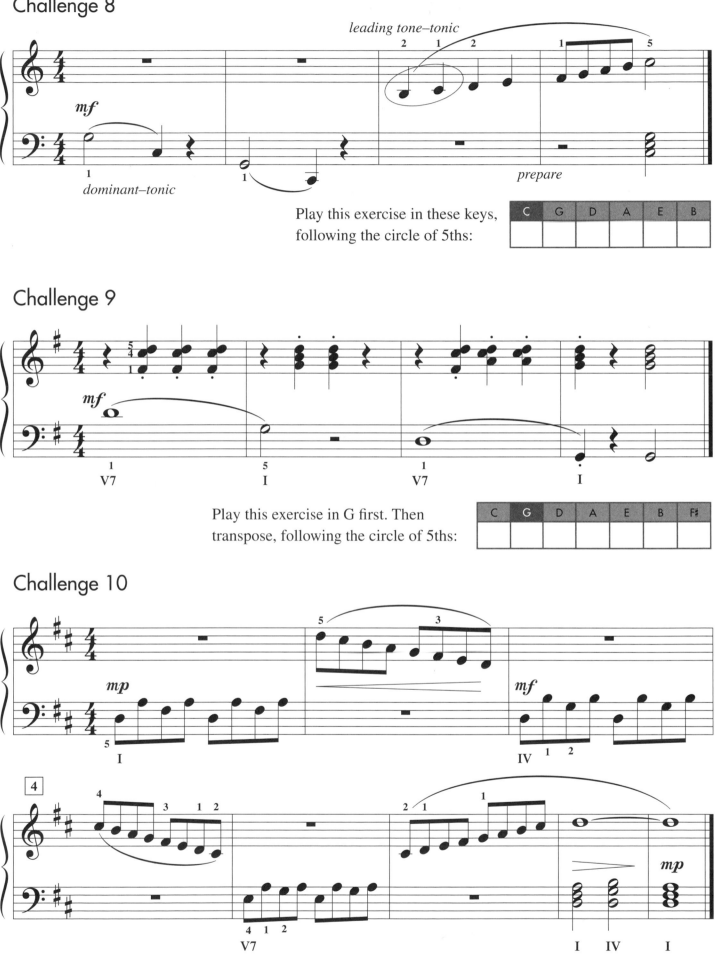

Play this exercise in these keys, following the circle of 5ths:

C	G	D	A	E	B

Challenge 9

Play this exercise in G first. Then transpose, following the circle of 5ths:

C	G	D	A	E	B	F#

Challenge 10

Play this exercise in D first. Then transpose, following the circle of 5ths:

C	G	D	A	E	B

1-Octave Major Flat Scales

Memorize each Scale Routine and play without stopping.

Put a ✔ next to each tempo as you build speed.

_____ ♩= 96   _____ ♩= 144   _____ ♩= 192

F Major Scale

Parallel motion

Contrary motion

Primary chords

I   IV   I   V7   I

Challenge 11

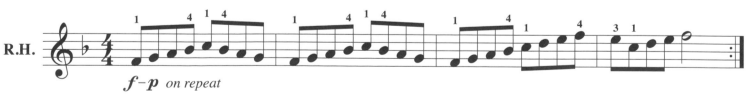

f–p on repeat

f–p on repeat

FF302

To name a flat key signature, find the *next-to-the-last* flat.
The name of that flat is the name of the key.

_____ ♩ = 96   _____ ♩ = 144   _____ ♩ = 192

B♭ Major Scale

R.H. fingering: Thumb falls on C and F for all flat key scales.

L.H. fingering: Group three plus four — **3-2-1** and **4-3-2-1**

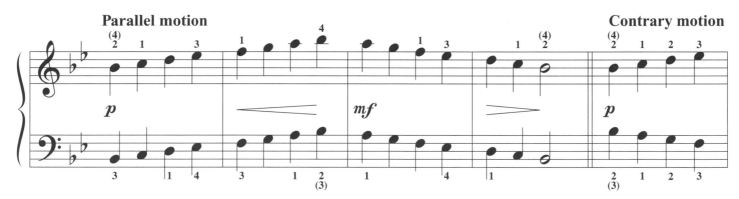

Parallel motion   **Contrary motion**

Primary chords

I   IV   I   V7   I

Challenge 12

This L.H. trill exercise builds on the **root**, **3rd**, and **5th** of the I chord.
Notice the "lower neighbor" is a half step below.

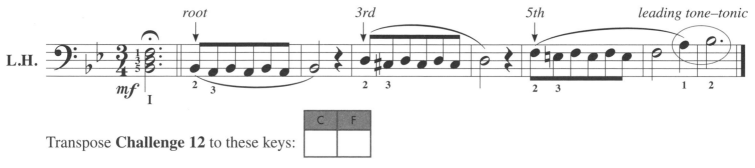

root   3rd   5th   leading tone–tonic

Transpose **Challenge 12** to these keys:

C	F

What is the name of the next-to-the-last flat? _____

That is the name of the key!

_____ ♩ = 96   _____ ♩ = 144   _____ ♩ = 192

E♭ Major Scale

R.H. fingering: Thumb falls on C and F for all flat key scales.

L.H. fingering: Group three plus four — **3-2-1** and **4-3-2-1**

Parallel motion   **Contrary motion**

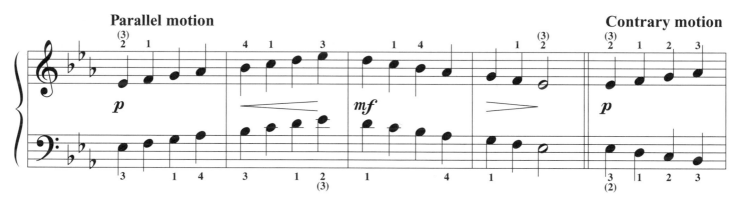

Primary chords

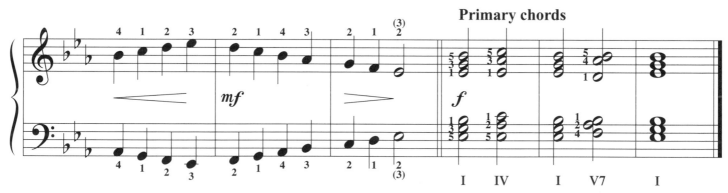

I   IV   I   V7   I

Challenge 13

dominant   –   tonic

Transpose **Challenge 13** to these keys:

C	F	B♭

16

A♭ Major Scale

R.H. fingering: Thumb falls on C and F for all flat key scales.

L.H. fingering: Group three plus four — **3-2-1** and **4-3-2-1**

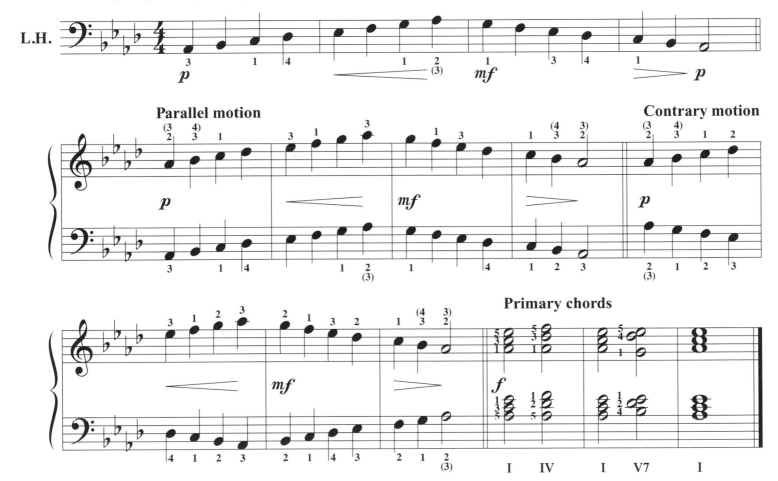

Parallel motion

Contrary motion

Primary chords

I   IV   I   V7   I

Challenge 14

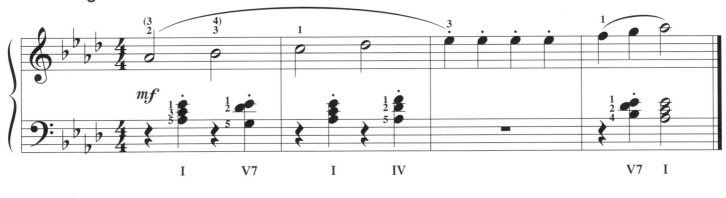

I   V7   I   IV   V7   I

Transpose **Challenge 14**:

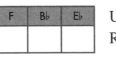

Use the appropriate R.H. fingering for each scale.
Remember thumb on C and F.

What is the name of the next-to-the-last flat? _____
That is the name of the key!

_____ ♩ = 96   _____ ♩ = 144   _____ ♩ = 192

D♭ Major Scale

R.H. fingering: Thumb falls on C and F for all flat key scales.

L.H. fingering: Group three plus four — **3-2-1** and **4-3-2-1**

Parallel motion   **Contrary motion**

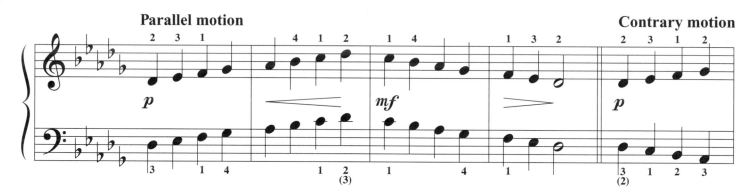

Primary chords

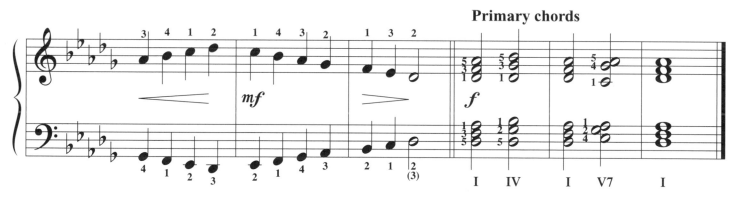

Challenge 15

Shift and use the D♭ scale fingering.   *dominant–tonic*

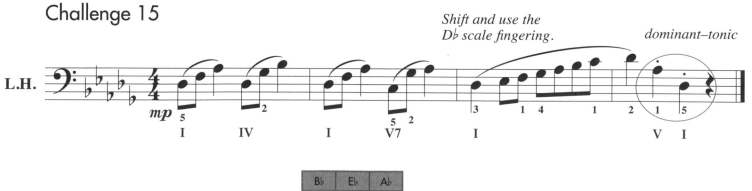

Transpose **Challenge 15** to these keys:

B♭	E♭	A♭

FF3025

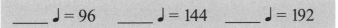 ♩ = 96 ____ ♩ = 144 ____ ♩ = 192

G♭ Major Scale

R.H. fingering: Now the thumb falls on the C♭ and the F keys.

L.H. fingering: Now group four plus three: **4-3-2-1** and **3-2-1**

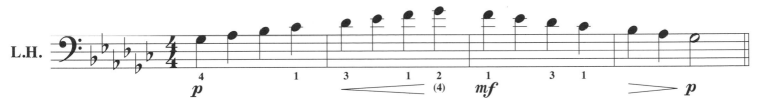

Parallel motion   **Contrary motion**

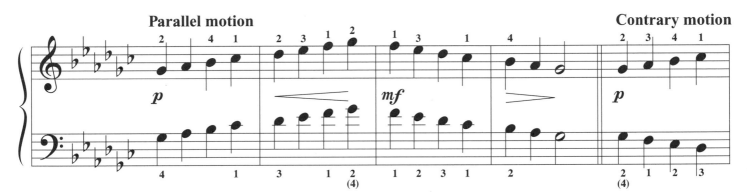

Primary chords

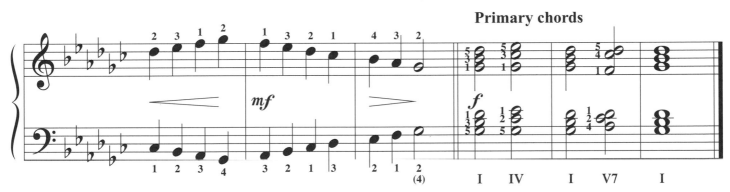

Challenge 16

Drop in with arm weight and release with a wrist float-off.

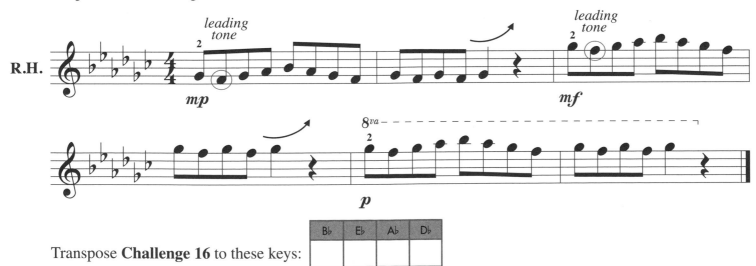

Transpose **Challenge 16** to these keys:

B♭	E♭	A♭	D♭

19

1-Octave Major Arpeggios

Arpeggio comes from the Italian word for "harp."
For an *arpeggio*, play the **notes of a chord** one after another, up or down the keyboard.

R.H. Technique Tips:

- Use a circular "under-and-over" wrist motion.
  This distributes the arm weight and relaxes the thumb.

- Notice the fingering is **1-2-3-5**.

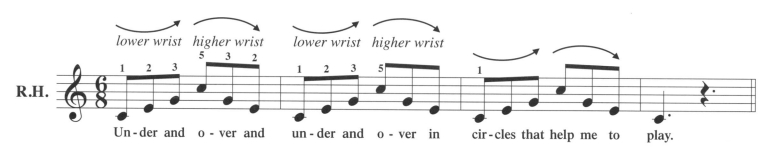

R.H.

Un-der and o-ver and   un-der and o-ver in   cir-cles that help me to   play.

- Use "under-and-over" wrist circles for each arpeggio.
- Memorize the **circle of 5ths** pattern.

Major Arpeggios for R.H.

Around the Circle of 5ths

C Major   F Major

B♭ Major   E♭ Major

A♭ Major   D♭ Major

20

FF3025

F♯ Major

B Major

E Major

A Major

D Major

G Major

C Major

Challenge 17

C Major

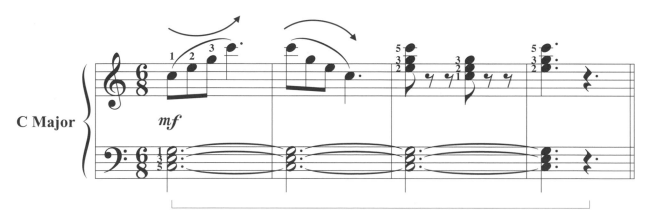

- Transpose **Challenge 17** to all keys, moving down chromatically:

C	B	B♭	A	A♭	G	F♯	F	E	E♭	D	D♭	C

- Can you play this exercise around the circle of 5ths?

C	F	B♭	E♭	A♭	D♭	F♯	B	E	A	D	G	C

L.H. Technique Tips:

- The L.H. wrist circle is the mirror image of the R.H. circle.
  Use a circular "over-and-under" wrist motion.

- There are two L.H. fingerings.
  Arpeggios with only white keys use **5-4-2-1**.

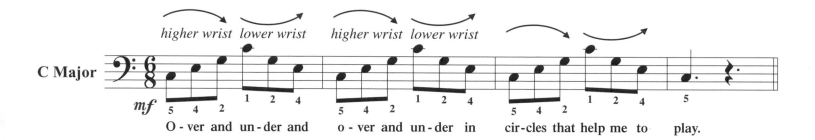

Major arpeggios with black keys use **5-3-2-1**.

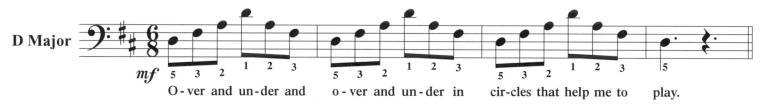

Major Arpeggios for L.H.

Around the Circle of 5ths

- In these patterns, the direction of the arpeggio is reversed
  from the example above. Use a circular "under-and-over"
  wrist motion for each.

- Notice the **circle of 5ths** pattern.

FF3025

A♭ Major

D♭ Major

F♯ Major

B Major

E Major

A Major

D Major

G Major

C Major

Challenge 18

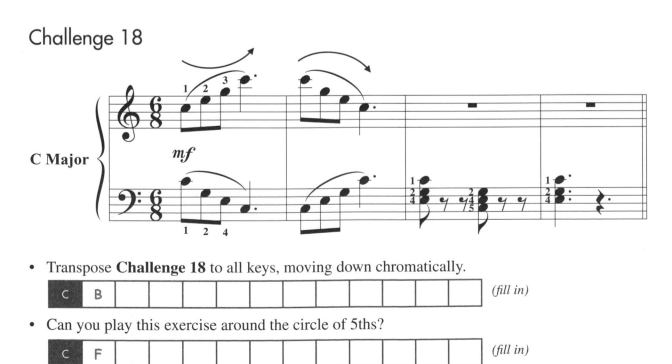

C Major

mf

- Transpose **Challenge 18** to all keys, moving down chromatically.

C	B											

(fill in)

- Can you play this exercise around the circle of 5ths?

C	F											

(fill in)

1-Octave Minor Flat Scales

Notice the three forms of the minor scale: *natural, harmonic,* and *melodic.*
Memorize this Scale Routine and play straight through.

Put a ✔ next to each tempo as you build speed.

_____ ♩ = 60 _____ ♩ = 80 _____ ♩ = 96

A Minor Scale
Hands Alone

A natural minor

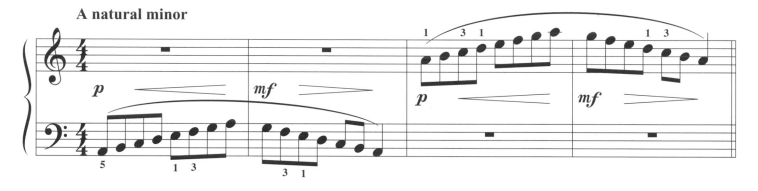

A harmonic minor

A melodic minor

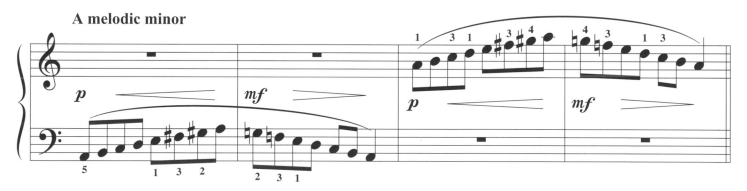

Primary chords

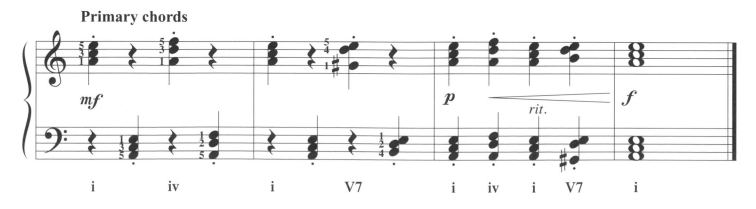

i   iv   i   V7   i   iv   i   V7   i

FF3025

Learn to play the Mini Etude without stopping.

_____ ♩ = 60 _____ ♩ = 80 _____ ♩ = 96

Mini Etude
Hands Together

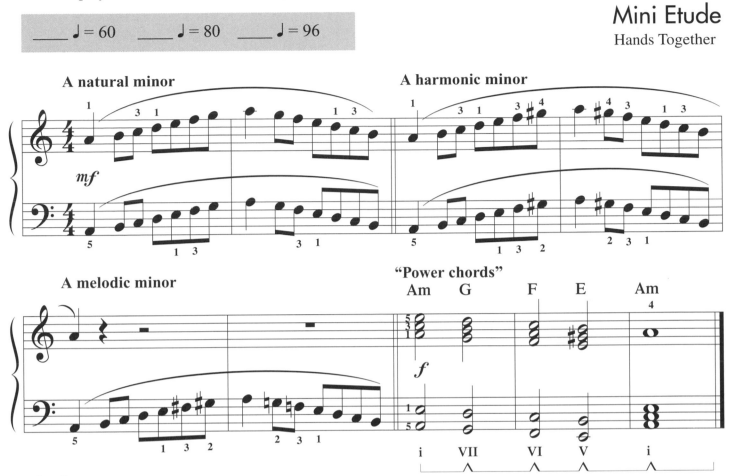

A natural minor

A harmonic minor

A melodic minor

"Power chords"
Am   G   F   E   Am

Challenge 19

Now play the scales of the Mini Etude s-l-o-w-l-y using this rhythm and articulation.
Play the "power chords" as written.

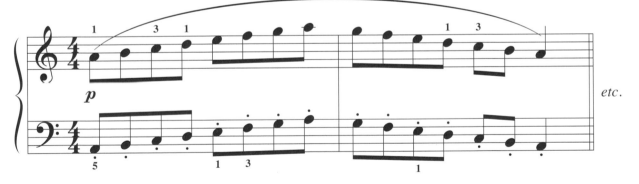

etc.

Challenge 20

Now play the Mini Etude using this two-note slur articulation.
Hint: Play the second note of each slur softer.

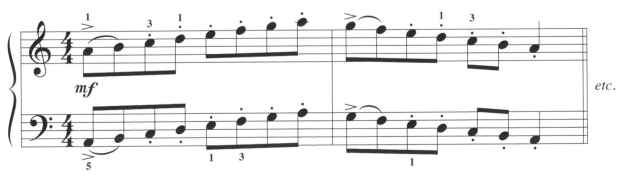

etc.

FF3025

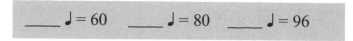

_____ ♩= 60   _____ ♩= 80   _____ ♩= 96

D Minor Scale
Hands Alone

D natural minor

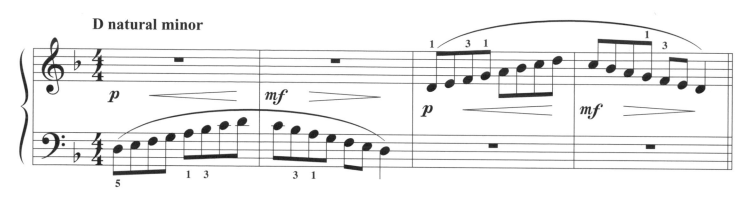

D harmonic minor

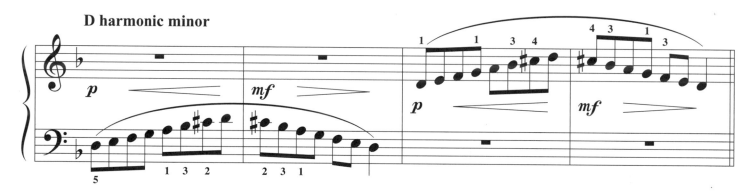

D melodic minor

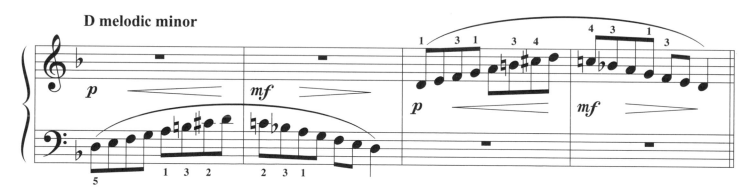

Primary chords

i   iv   i   V7   i   iv   i   V7   i

26

Hands Together

_____ ♩ = 60   _____ ♩ = 80   _____ ♩ = 96

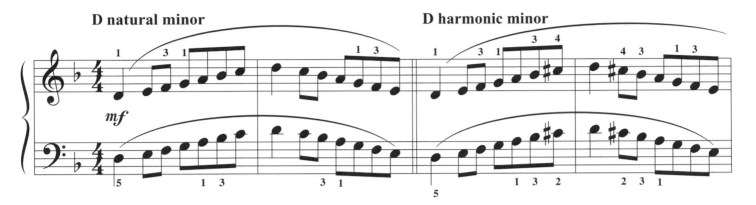

D natural minor   **D harmonic minor**

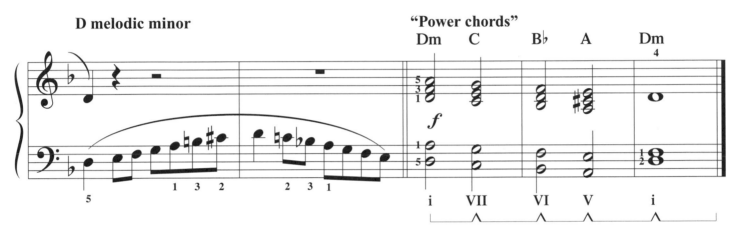

D melodic minor   **"Power chords"**

Tarantella*

Frank Lynes
(1858–1913, U.S.)

Challenge 21

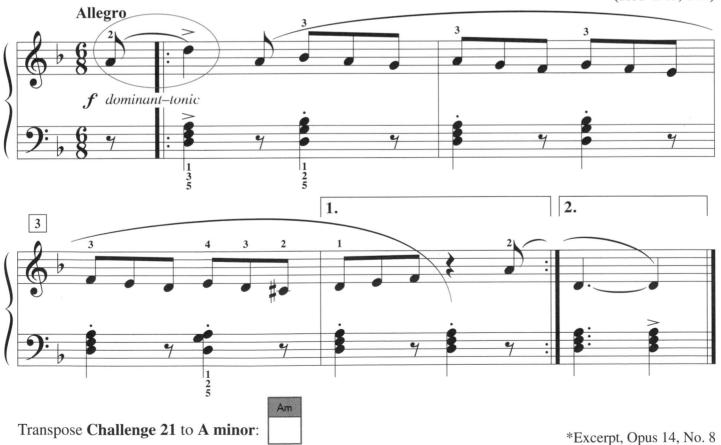

Transpose **Challenge 21** to **A minor**: | Am |

*Excerpt, Opus 14, No. 8

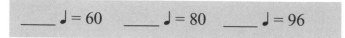

____ ♩ = 60   ____ ♩ = 80   ____ ♩ = 96

G Minor Scale
Hands Alone

G natural minor

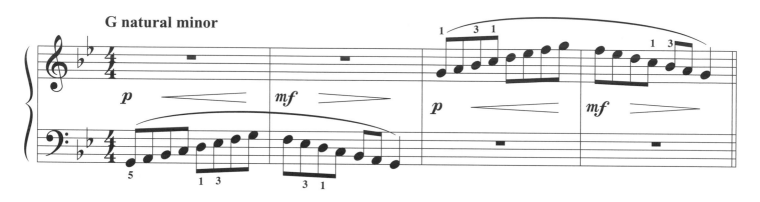

G harmonic minor

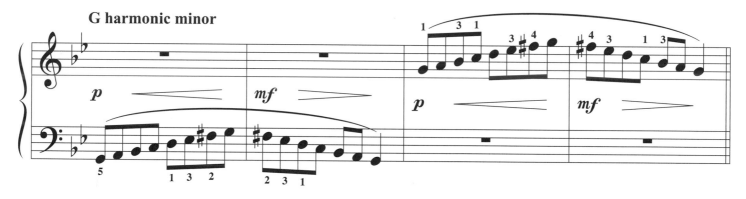

G melodic minor

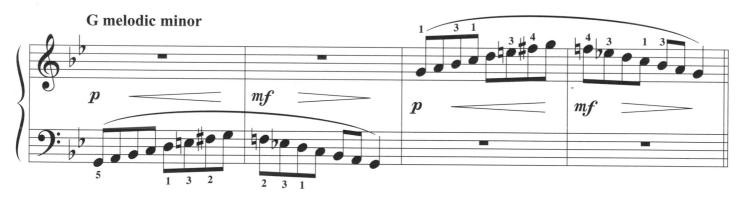

Primary chords

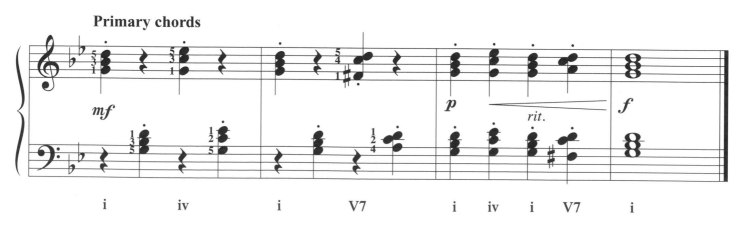

i   iv   i   V7   i   iv   i V7   i

28

_____ ♩ = 60   _____ ♩ = 80   _____ ♩ = 96

Mini Etude
Hands Together

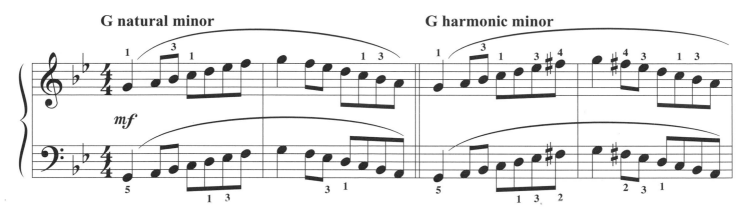

G natural minor   G harmonic minor

_mf_

G melodic minor   "Power chords"
                         Gm   F   E♭   D   Gm

_f_

i   VII   VI   V   i

Baroque Air*

Challenge 22

Daniel Speer
(1636–1709, Germany)

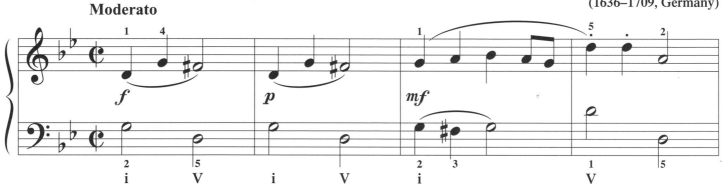

Moderato

_f_   _p_   _mf_

i   V   i   V   i   V

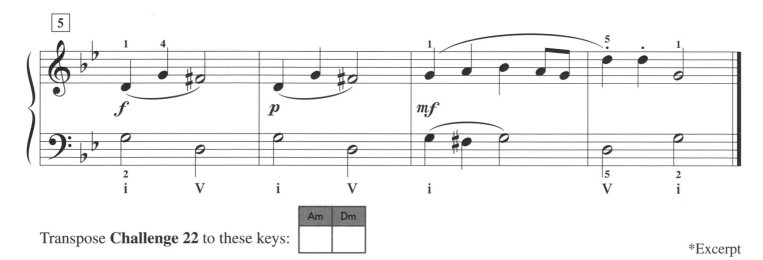

5

_f_   _p_   _mf_

i   V   i   V   i   V   i

Transpose **Challenge 22** to these keys:

Am	Dm

*Excerpt

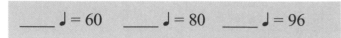

C Minor Scale
Hands Alone

C natural minor

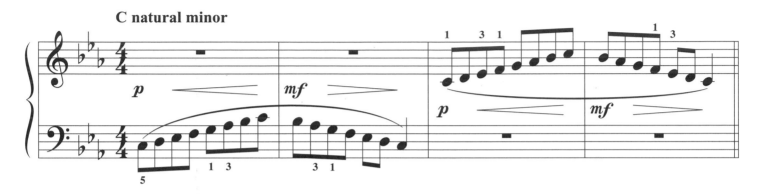

C harmonic minor

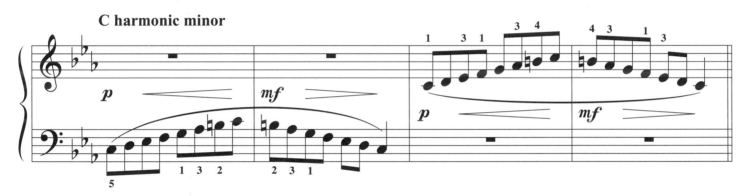

C melodic minor

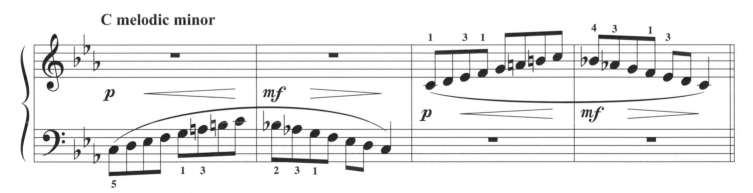

Primary chords

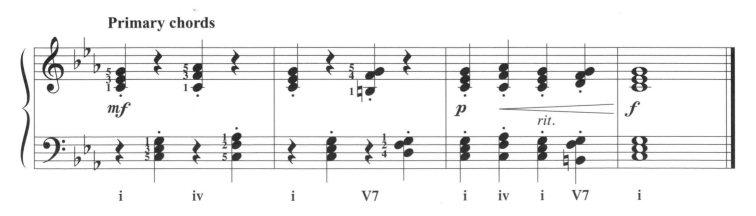

i   iv   i   V7   i   iv   i   V7   i

Mini Etude
Hands Together

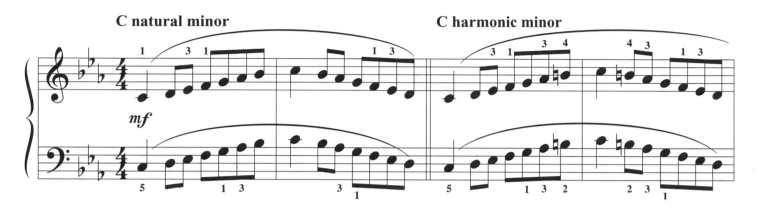

C natural minor   **C harmonic minor**

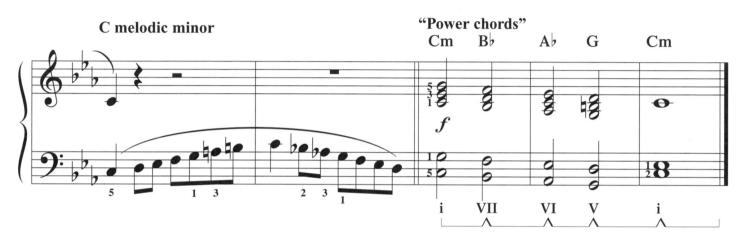

C melodic minor   **"Power chords"**

Challenge 23

What form of the minor scale is used?

A Growing Wind

N. Faber

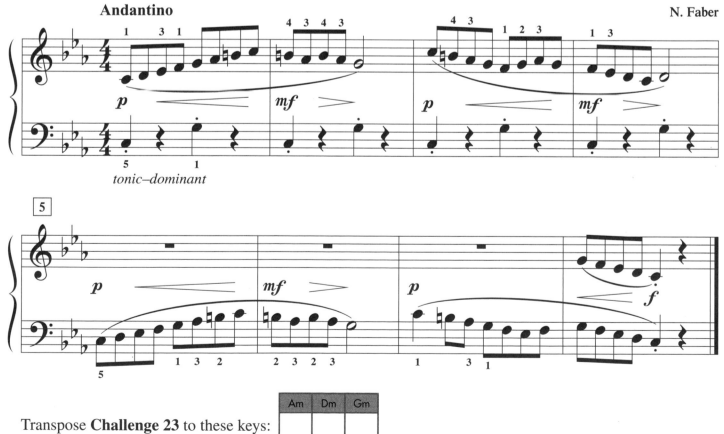

tonic–dominant

Transpose **Challenge 23** to these keys:

Am	Dm	Gm

F Minor Scale
Hands Alone

F natural minor

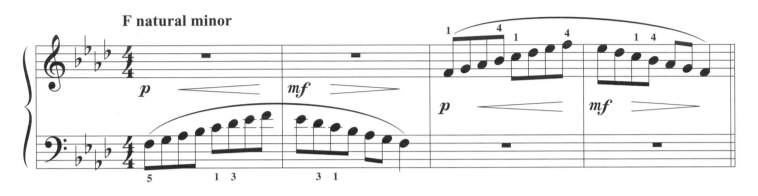

F harmonic minor

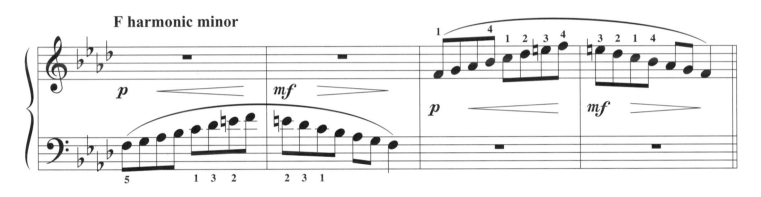

F melodic minor

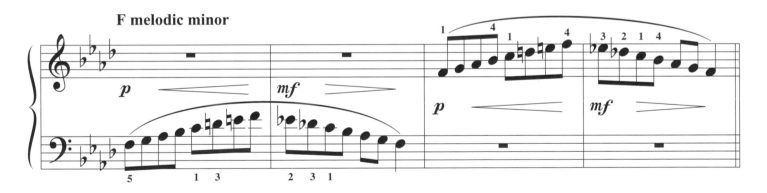

Primary chords

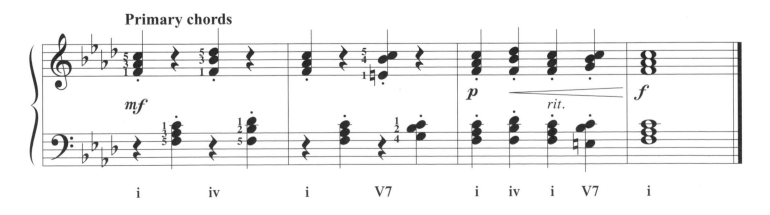

i   iv   i   V7   i   iv   i   V7   i

Mini Etude
Hands Together

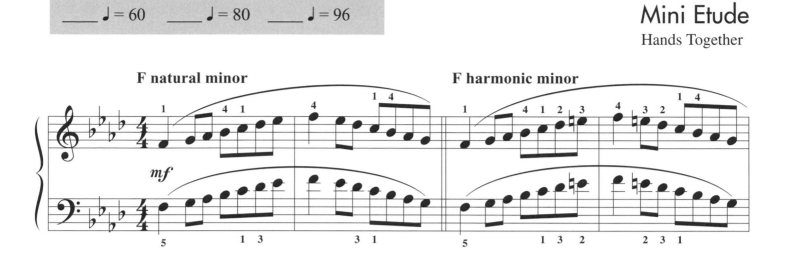

F natural minor

F harmonic minor

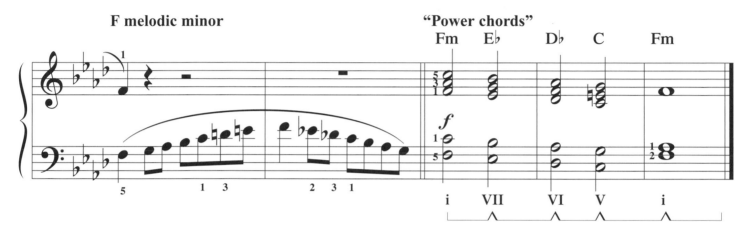

F melodic minor

"Power chords"

Challenge 24

Play the Mini Etude using this dotted rhythm pattern.

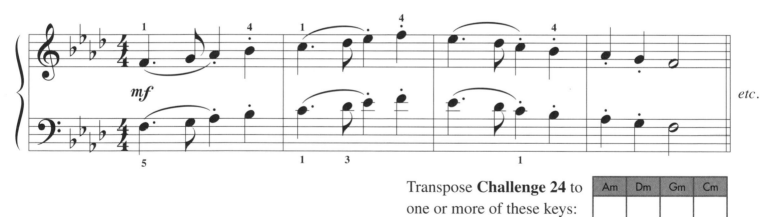

etc.

Transpose **Challenge 24** to one or more of these keys:

Am	Dm	Gm	Cm

Challenge 25

Now harmonize the scales using the i–iv chords. Play the chords *staccato*.

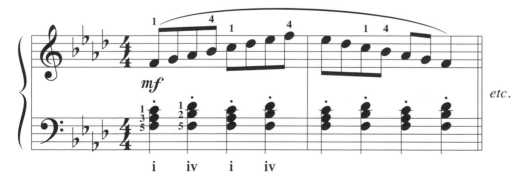

etc.

Transpose **Challenge 25** to one or more of these keys:

Am	Dm	Gm	Cm

i   iv   i   iv

_____ ♩= 60   _____ ♩= 80   _____ ♩= 96

B♭ Minor Scale
Hands Alone

B♭ natural minor

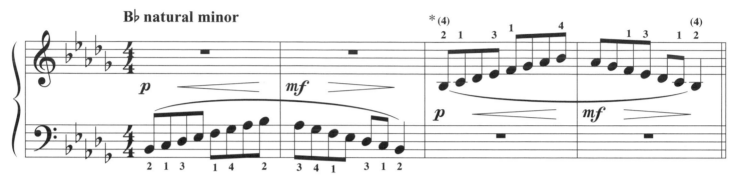

B♭ harmonic minor

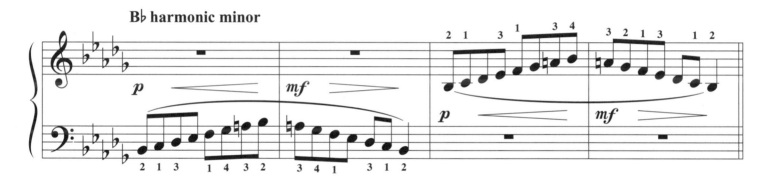

B♭ melodic minor

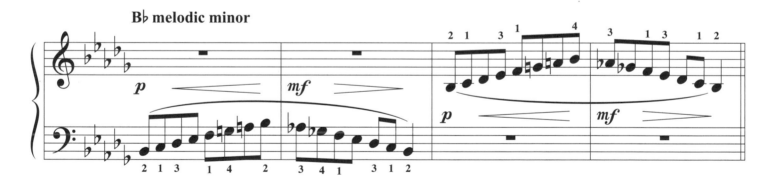

Primary chords

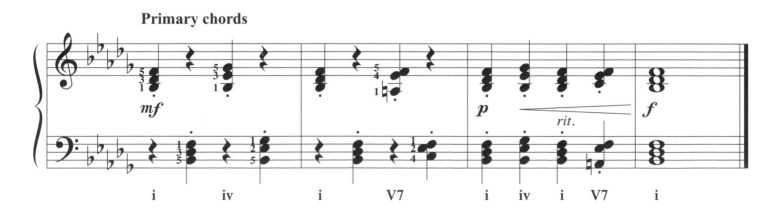

i   iv   i   V7   i   iv   i   V7   i

*Students may begin and end the R.H. scales with finger 4 as an alternate fingering.

Mini Etude
Hands Together

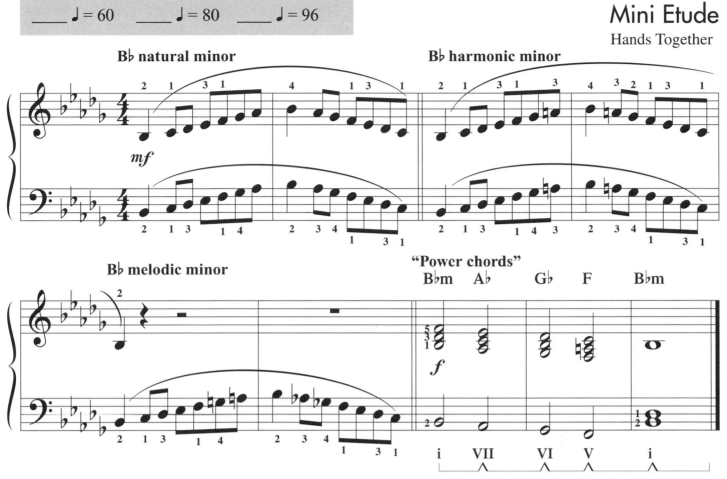

Challenge 26

Play the Mini Etude using this interlocking rhythm pattern. Play lightly and *staccato!*

Very steady

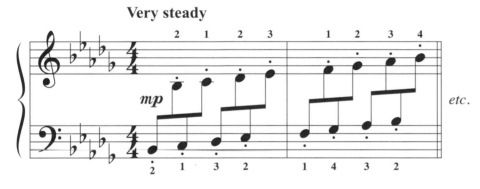

Transpose **Challenge 26** to one or more of these keys:

Dm	Gm	Cm	Fm

Challenge 27

Now play the Mini Etude using this dotted rhythm.

Boldly

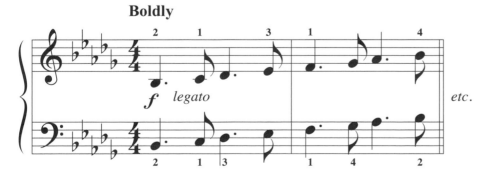

Transpose **Challenge 27** to one or more of these keys:

Dm	Gm	Cm	Fm

_____ ♩ = 60   _____ ♩ = 80   _____ ♩ = 96

E♭ Minor Scale
Hands Alone

E♭ natural minor

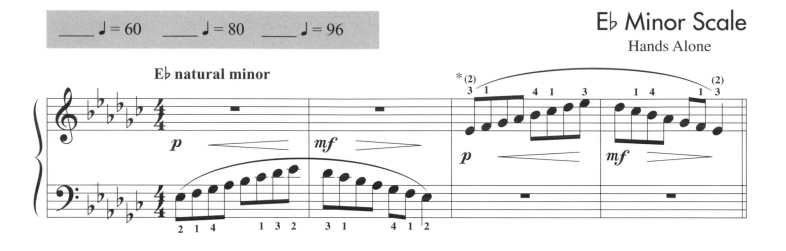

E♭ harmonic minor

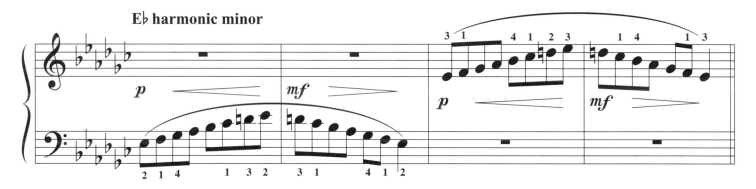

E♭ melodic minor

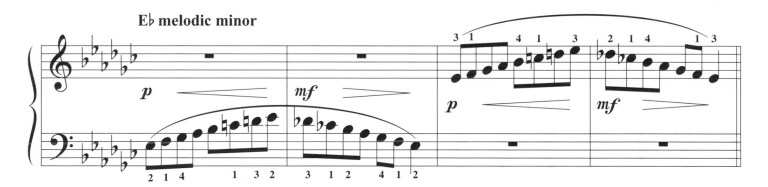

Primary chords

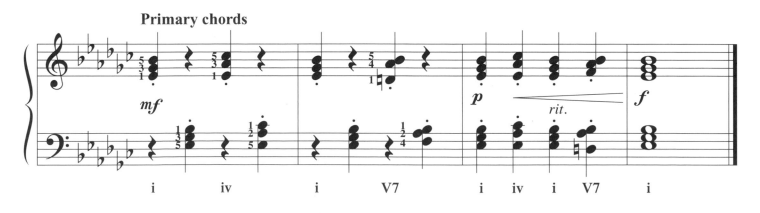

i   iv   i   V7   i   iv   i   V7   i

*Students may begin and end the R.H. scales with finger 2 as an alternate fingering.

FF3025

_____ ♩ = 60   _____ ♩ = 80   _____ ♩ = 96

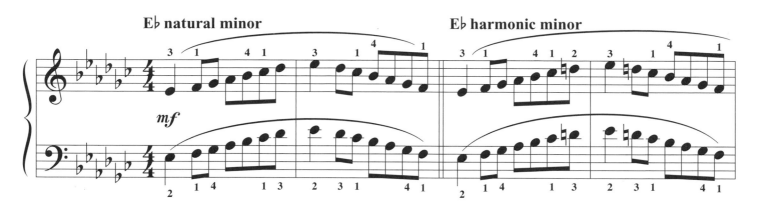

E♭ natural minor   E♭ harmonic minor

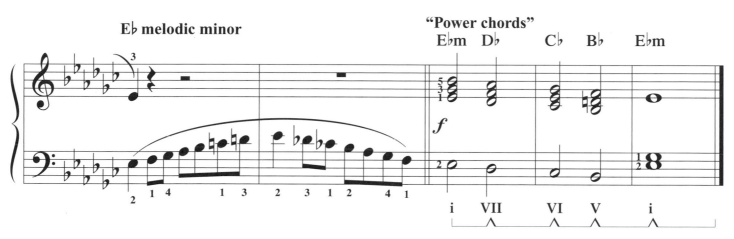

E♭ melodic minor   "Power chords"
E♭m   D♭   C♭   B♭   E♭m

i   VII   VI   V   i

Challenge 28

• Play this Alberti bass exercise listening for smooth chord changes.

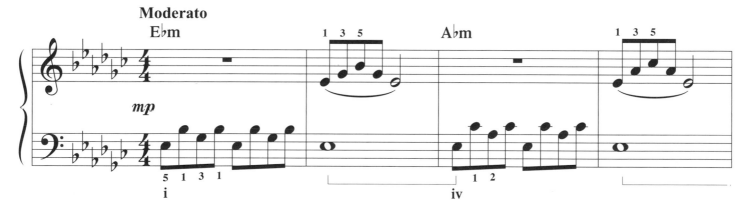

Moderato
E♭m   A♭m
i   iv

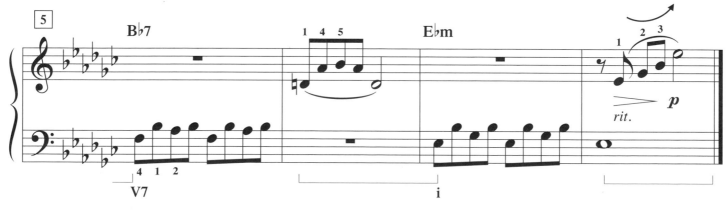

B♭7   E♭m
V7   i

Gm	Cm	Fm	B♭m

Transpose **Challenge 28** to one or more of these keys:

_____ ♩ = 60   _____ ♩ = 80   _____ ♩ = 96

E Minor Scale
Hands Alone

E natural minor

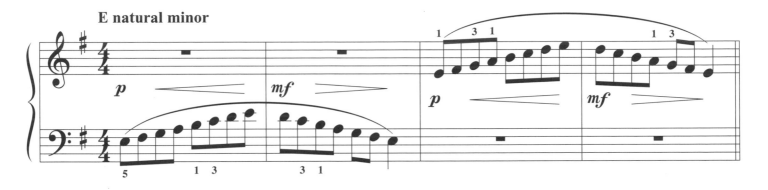

E harmonic minor

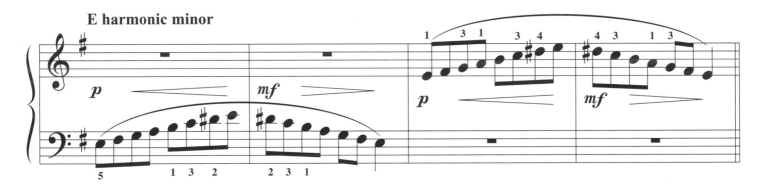

E melodic minor

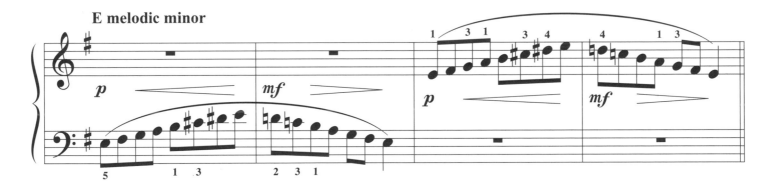

Primary chords

i   iv   i   V7   i   iv   i   V7   i

FF302♯

Mini Etude
Hands Together

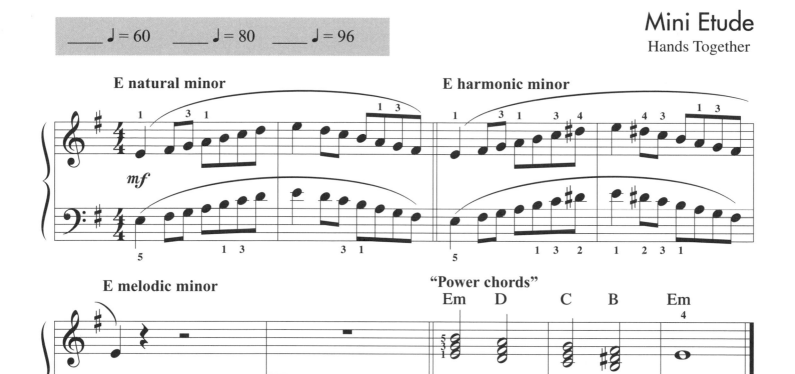

Challenge 29

Notice the chord letter names above the staff.
Notice the Roman numerals below the staff.

Greensleeves

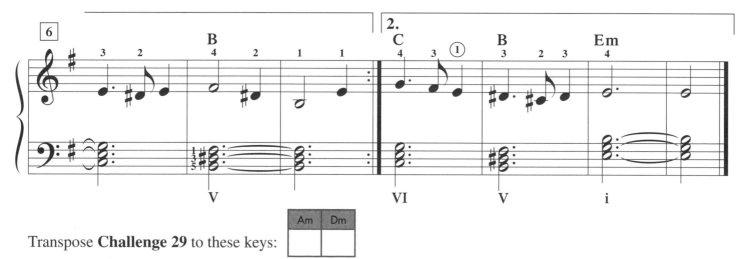

Transpose **Challenge 29** to these keys:

Am	Dm

_____ ♩ = 60   _____ ♩ = 80   _____ ♩ = 96

B Minor Scale
Hands Alone

B natural minor

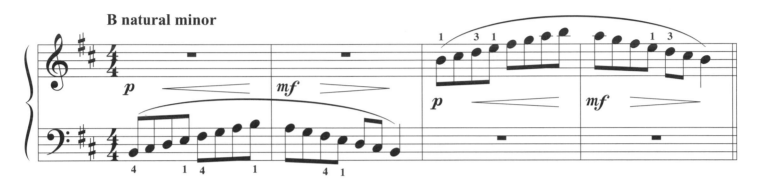

B harmonic minor

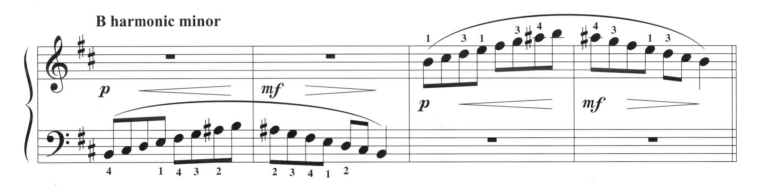

B melodic minor

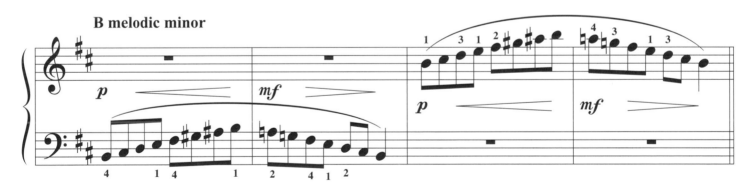

Primary chords

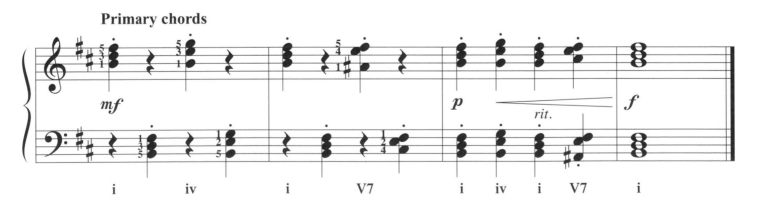

i   iv   i   V7   i   iv   i   V7   i

FF302

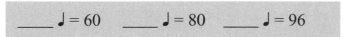

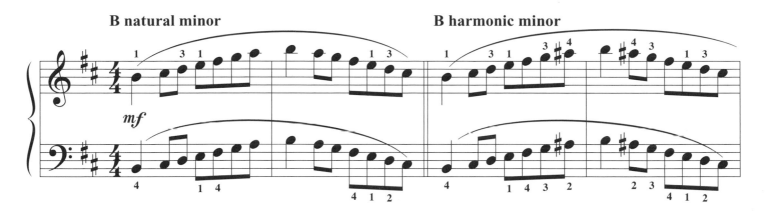

B natural minor

B harmonic minor

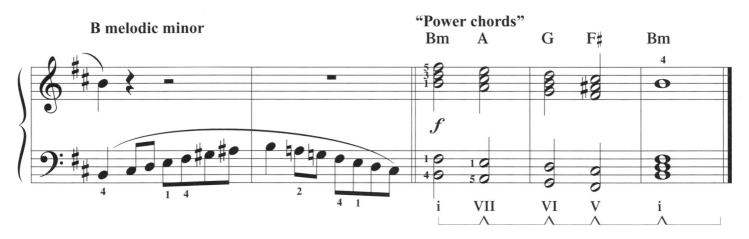

B melodic minor

"Power chords"

Bm   A   G   F♯   Bm

i   VII   VI   V   i

Challenge 30

In the chord progression below, the "power chords" are followed by the primary chords.

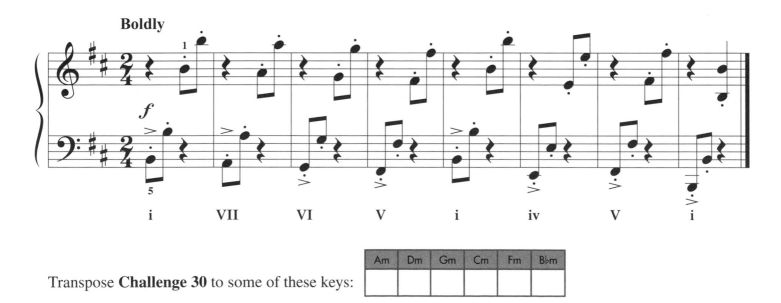

Boldly

i   VII   VI   V   i   iv   V   i

Am	Dm	Gm	Cm	Fm	B♭m

Transpose **Challenge 30** to some of these keys:

_____ ♩ = 60 _____ ♩ = 80 _____ ♩ = 96

F# Minor Scale
Hands Alone

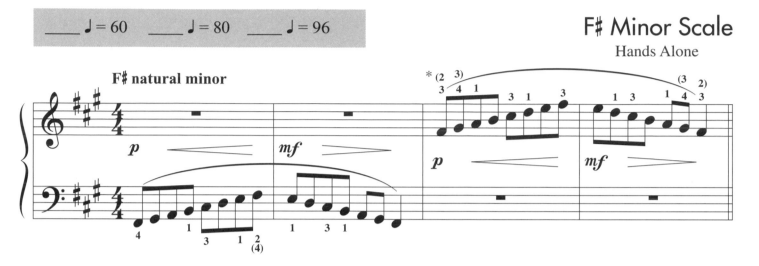

F# natural minor

*(2 3)

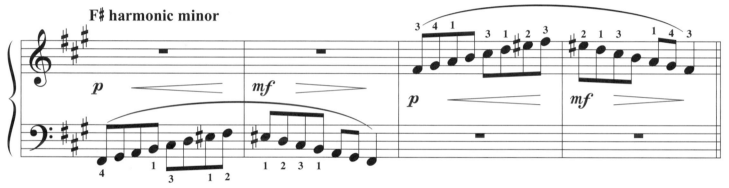

F# harmonic minor

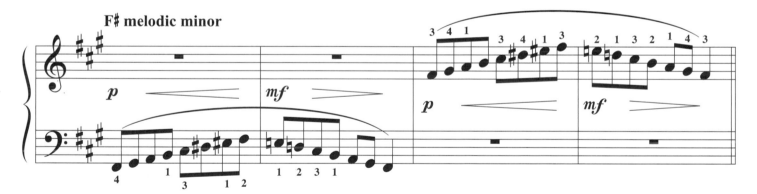

F# melodic minor

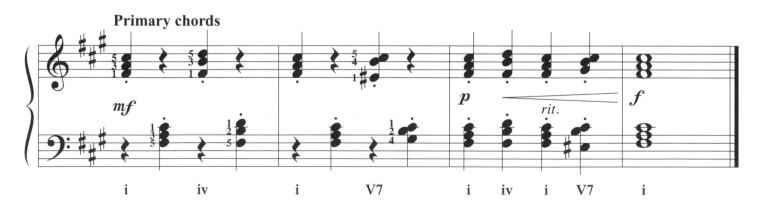

Primary chords

i   iv   i   V7   i   iv   i   V7   i

*Students may begin and end the R.H. scales with 2-3 as an alternate fingering.

FF3025

_____ ♩ = 60   _____ ♩ = 80   _____ ♩ = 96

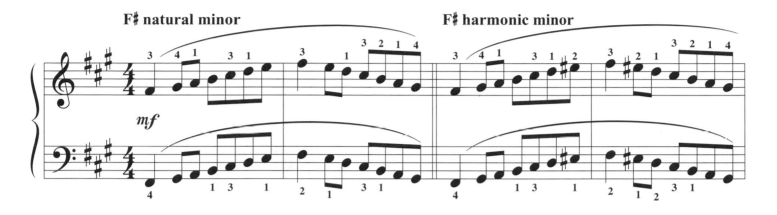

F♯ natural minor

F♯ harmonic minor

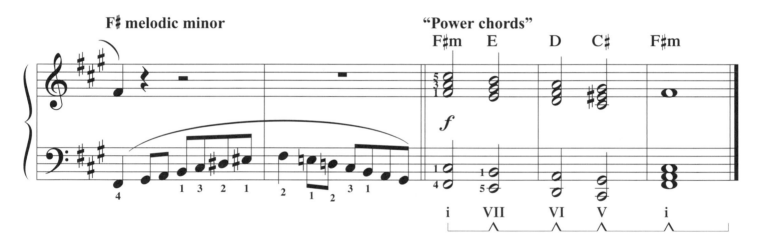

F♯ melodic minor

"Power chords"

Challenge 31

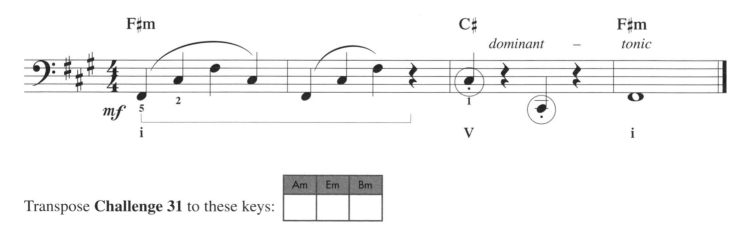

Transpose **Challenge 31** to these keys:

Am	Em	Bm

_____ ♩ = 60 _____ ♩ = 80 _____ ♩ = 96

C♯ Minor Scale
Hands Alone

C♯ natural minor

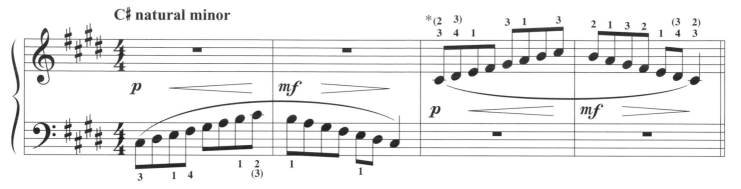

C♯ harmonic minor

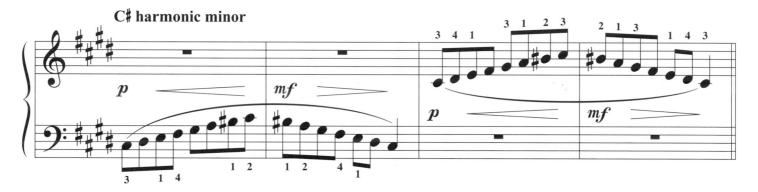

C♯ melodic minor

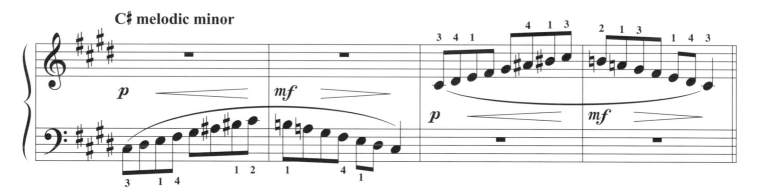

Primary chords

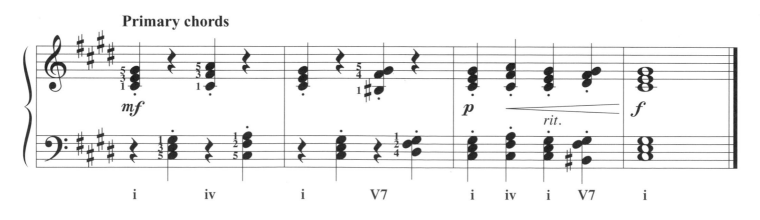

i   iv   i   V7   i   iv   i   V7   i

*Students may begin and end the R.H. scales with 2-3 as an alternate fingering.

FF302

Mini Etude
Hands Together

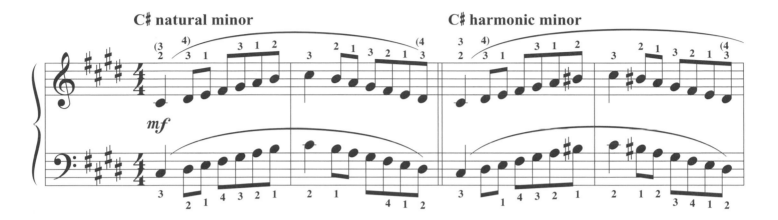

C♯ natural minor   C♯ harmonic minor

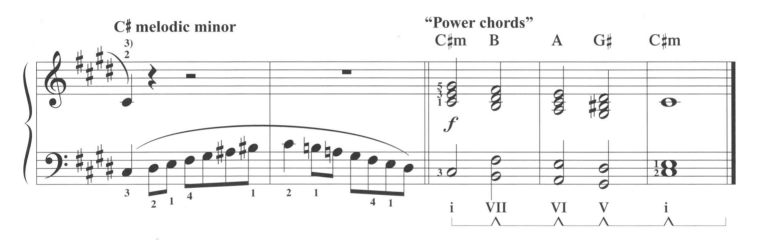

C♯ melodic minor   "Power chords"
C♯m   B   A   G♯   C♯m

i   VII   VI   V   i

Challenge 32

This R.H. trill exercise builds on the **root**, **3rd**, and **5th** of the i chord.
Notice the "lower neighbor" is a half step below.

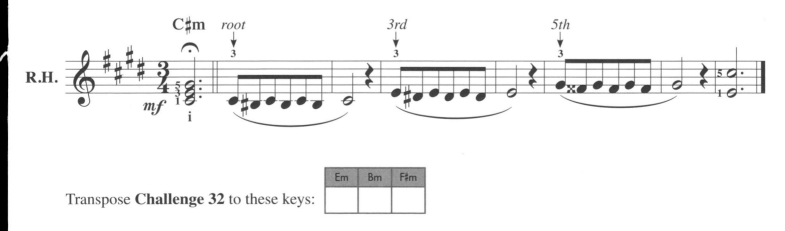

C♯m _root_   _3rd_   _5th_

R.H.

Em	Bm	F♯m

Transpose **Challenge 32** to these keys:

_____ ♩ = 60   _____ ♩ = 80   _____ ♩ = 96

G♯ Minor Scale
Hands Alone

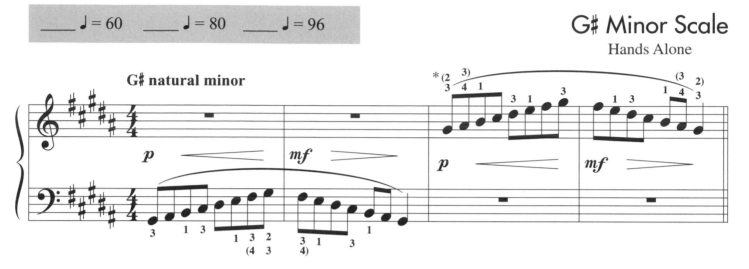

G♯ natural minor

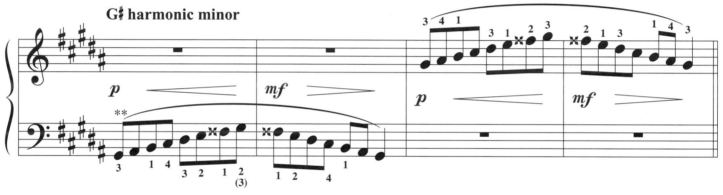

G♯ harmonic minor

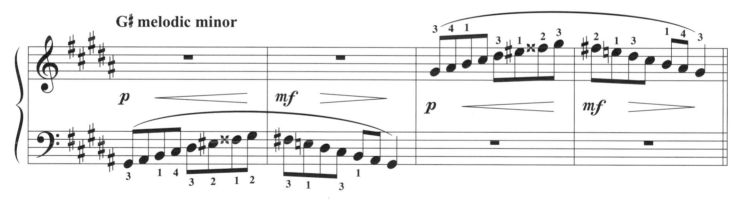

G♯ melodic minor

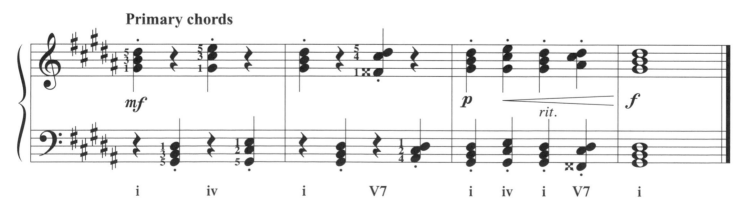

Primary chords

i   iv   i   V7   i   iv   i   V7   i

*Students may begin and end the R.H. scales with 2-3 as an alternate fingering.

** This is the only scale where the L.H. fingering in the harmonic minor is different from the natural minor.

____ ♩ = 60   ____ ♩ = 80   ____ ♩ = 96

G♯ natural minor   **G♯ harmonic minor**

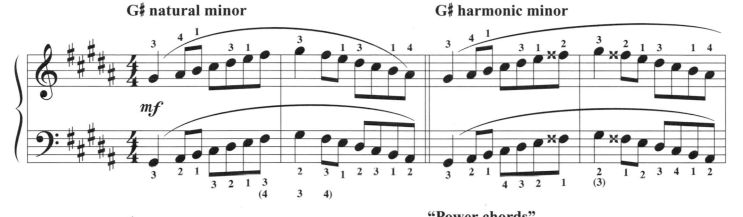

G♯ melodic minor   **"Power chords"**

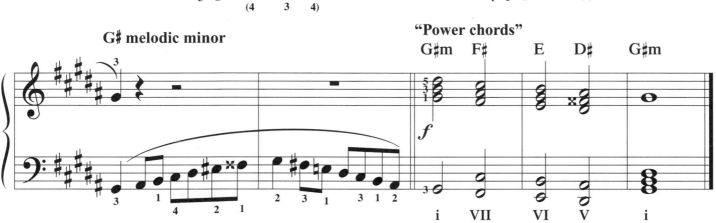

Challenge 33

This scale exercise centers around
the *tonic* and *dominant* scale degrees.

Scale Swirls

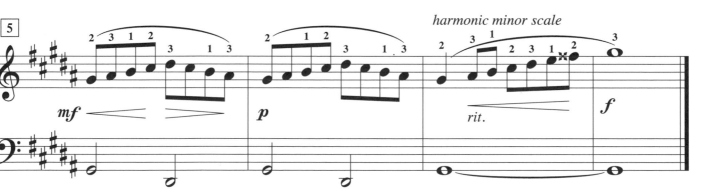

Transpose **Challenge 33** to these keys:

F♯m	C♯m

SECTION 6
1-Octave Minor Arpeggios

These minor arpeggios are presented *chromatically* (going up by half steps).

Technique Tips:
- Use a circular "under-and-over" wrist motion to distribute the arm weight.
- Relax the thumb and let the hand close.

Minor Arpeggios for R.H.

FF30

Challenge 34

Transpose this exercise to all minor keys, moving *down* chromatically.

Technique Tip:
Remember to use the "under-and-over"
wrist circles to relax the hand.

Minor Arpeggios for L.H.

C minor

Low wrist ris - ing, un - der and o - ver and un - der and off.

C# minor

D minor

Eb minor

E minor

F minor

Challenge 35

Transpose this exercise to all minor keys, moving *down* chromatically.

Chord Progressions and Harmony

I, IV, and V chords are known as the primary chords, but the **vi** chord (minor) is also vital.

Play these four **chord progressions** straight through.
Note that the last two patterns are the basis of many pop songs.

Pop Chord Etude

Memorize this etude and
transpose to many keys:

C	G	D	A	E	B	F	Bb	Eb	Ab	Db	F# / Gb

FF302

Challenge 36

Use this variation as you play and transpose the last two chord progressions on page 52 (measures 9-17).

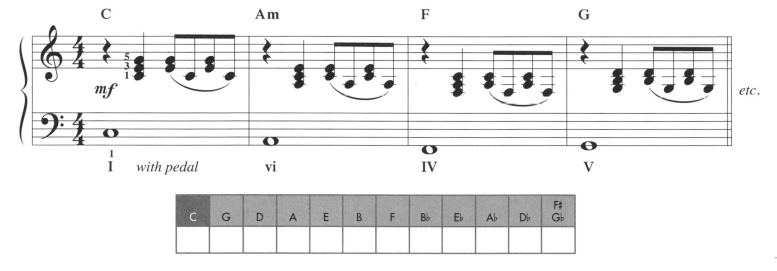

C	G	D	A	E	B	F	B♭	E♭	A♭	D♭	F#/G♭

"Power Chord" Etude

This minor-key chord progression utilizes the "power chords" you have learned. Transpose to many keys!

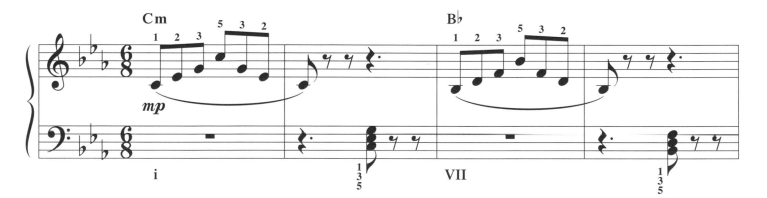

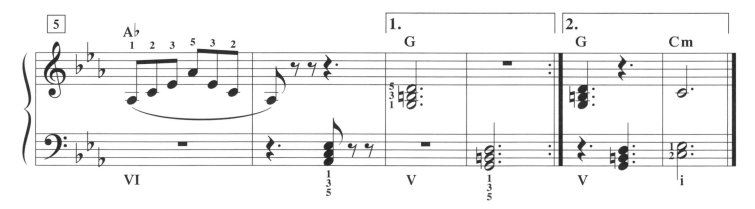

Cm	Dm	Em	Fm	Gm	Am	Bm

C#m	E♭m	F#m	G#m	B♭m

"Classic" Cadence

C Major

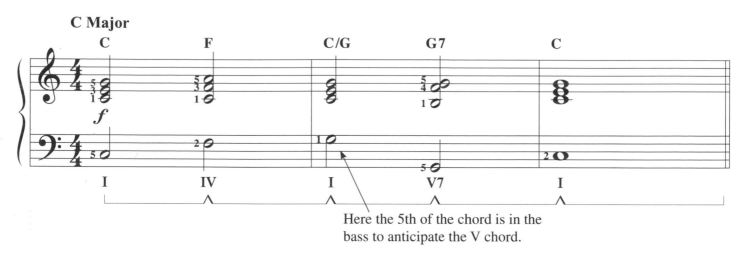

Here the 5th of the chord is in the bass to anticipate the V chord.

Play in all
12 keys:

C	Db	D	Eb	E	F	F#	G	Ab	A	Bb	B

Now use this two-hand accompaniment pattern for the above.

Challenge 37

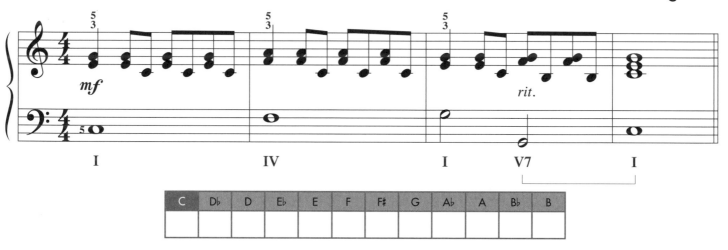

C	Db	D	Eb	E	F	F#	G	Ab	A	Bb	B

For a stepwise bass line (scale degrees 3-4-5), begin with the 3rd in the bass.

Challenge 38

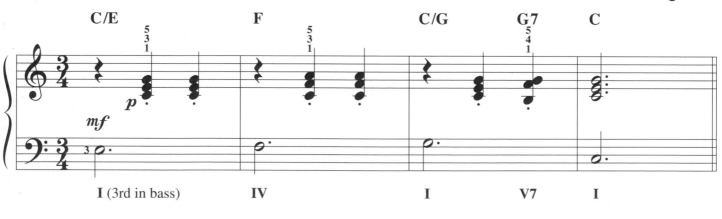

C	Db	D	Eb	E	F	F#	G	Ab	A	Bb	B

Happy Birthday

Memorize the harmony of this famous melody
and play it in all 12 keys.

Harmony

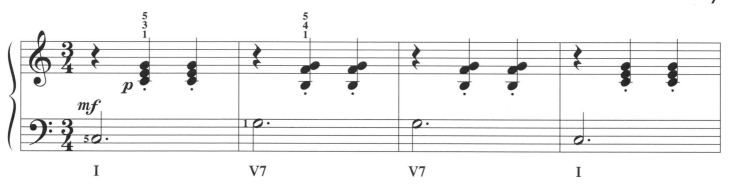

I   V7   V7   I

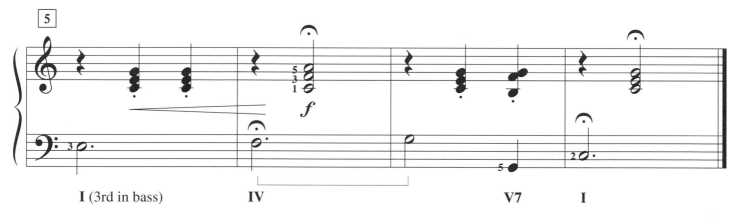

I (3rd in bass)   IV   V7   I

C	G	D	A	E	B	F	B♭	E♭	A♭	D♭	F# G♭

Now try it with the melody in the R.H. and the harmony in the L.H.
Play it in your favorite keys!

Melody

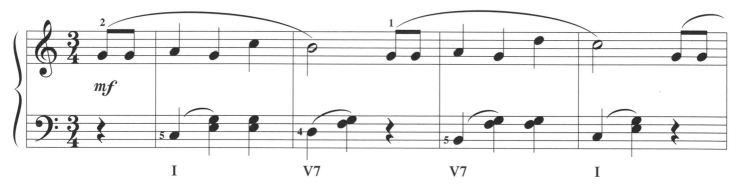

I   V7   V7   I

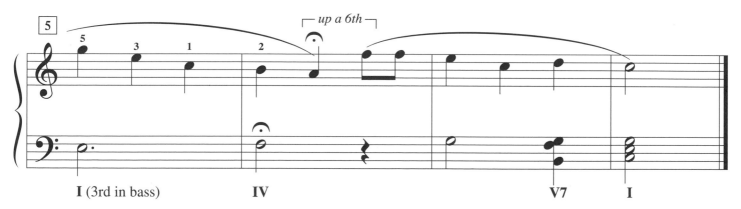

I (3rd in bass)   IV   V7   I

Certificate
of Achievement

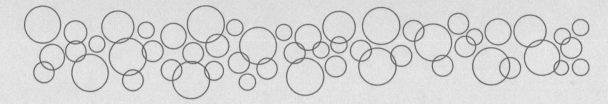

CONGRATULATIONS TO

•———————————————————————————————•

You have completed

PIANO ADVENTURES® SCALE BOOK 2

You are now ready for

PIANO ADVENTURES® SCALE BOOK 3

Keep up the good work!

•———————————————————————————————•

Teacher

•———————————————————————————————•

Date